PRAYERS FOR YOUR WAYWARD SPOUSE

MK Clark

Audie House Publishing

This book is dedicated to Shona, Lauren, Ashley and Kelly. Thank you for praying for me so I could pray for my husband.

CONTENTS

Title Page

Copyright

Dedication

Who Is This Book For?   1

Your Unique Position To Intercede   4

How To Be In Covenant With God   9

Prayers For Your Wayward Spouse   12

Have Grace For Yourself, You Need It!   32

Resources   40

About The Author   45

WHO IS THIS BOOK FOR?

You are not crazy to want to reconcile with a spouse who is wayward. You are not alone on this journey, regardless if you personally know people who have traveled this exact path. There is hope.

This book was written for anyone who has a spouse who has become wayward with them and with God. Be it through adultery, drug or alcohol addiction, pornography or the cultural lies of deconstructionism, if you have a marriage that is now unrecognizable, you need to know that there is hope for you, your spouse and your marriage.

My story is not unique, but when it began, I knew no one personally who had experienced the same chaos and confusion that I did. My husband had an emotional affair with a woman whom he saw on a regular basis, and this great marriage that I *thought* I had came to a screeching halt one day. He professed to be a Christian before the affair, but once he confessed the affair, he revealed that he wasn't sure he was really interested in following the God of the Bible.

Later I encountered other betrayed women, and one lamented that there were few books out there offering hope. Most of those that she had found were about picking up the pieces after the divorce. My book is an attempt to change that. Five years after my husband's disclosure of the affair, we are not immune from the effects of this trauma. But, we are committed to staying in our marriage and following God, obeying Him so we can live out the life and marriage He always intended for us to have. Seeing God as not just my Savior but also as my King makes the difference in how I live my life. My husband is coming to know that truth as well, working out his own salvation (Philippians 2:12). Our marriage could not be repaired if my husband did not turn back to God, and I believe these prayers were instrumental in his decision to do so.

I am not a theologian, Biblical scholar or ancient Hebrew and Greek linguist. If you want amazing Biblical commentary and language insight, you need to look elsewhere. I am just a woman who interceded through prayer for her husband and her marriage, and the three of us (him, me and our marriage) are still standing. The prayers I prayed are listed in this book for you to do the same for your spouse, your marriage and yourself.

Please know that this is not a "you must save your marriage at any cost" type of book. If your spouse has allowed you that choice and not taken it away by making the choice for himself, then the choice stays with you. If you choose to stay, then

2

consider these prayers the weapons you will use to fight the battle for justice and righteousness in your home. Think of these prayers as drowning out the voices (and therefore the effectiveness) of Pride, Fear, Selfishness, Adultery, Addiction and all the rest that work against you, your spouse and your marriage night and day. Your enemy, Satan (the Accuser) does not have a weapon to match, all he has is deception to make you *think* that he does.

I know that the majority of my readers will be wives desiring to intercede for their husbands. Because I am a woman who was betrayed by my husband, I refer to the spouse usually as a man. However, this book can be utilized just as easily by husbands who have been betrayed by their wives. In fact, I hope this book does find a following among betrayed husbands. More often, betrayed men are encouraged to make the automatic choice to divorce, leaving little room to overcome the trauma together with their wives. If you are a man reading this, may this book be the beginning step of your journey in the direction you decide to go, not where society tells you to go.

Remember friends, you are not crazy and you are not alone. There is hope!

YOUR UNIQUE POSITION TO INTERCEDE

Prayers Are Power

You and your prayers are the most powerful weapons in this fight for your spouse and your marriage. As a married couple you are considered as one in the eyes of God (Ephesians 5:31). Does that mean that if your spouse sins, you are responsible for his sins? No, not at all. But it does mean that you can intercede on his behalf, and God can hear you as he hears your spouse on your marriage. If my husband won't pray for his own journey back to God, I can pray about that for him. How seriously will God take the prayer of the other part of my husband crying out for him? Pretty seriously, I think. You are acting as the righteous half of your spouse, praying the things he doesn't or won't pray himself.

God's Covenants As A Picture Of Marriage

God chose Abraham and his descendants to represent Him on Earth to all of the other people groups by creating a covenant with Abraham. When Abraham's descendants through Jacob, now known as Israel, left Egypt led by Moses, God instituted another covenant with those descendants and gave them His law.

Throughout the Old Testament, God uses the picture of Israel as His bride (Isaiah 54:5, Jeremiah 31:32, Ezekiel 16:8) to describe His covenant relationship with Israel. God also describes the church as a bride for His son Jesus (Revelation 19:6-9, Ephesians 5:25-31). Both the covenant that God made with Israel via Moses and the last covenant that God made with believers through Jesus were made with blood sacrifices (young bulls in the first covenant and Jesus' own blood for the second one). Think about when a man and woman come together for marital relations for the first time–there is blood shed when that union is created. This is a picture of creating that covenant.

So, God is a God of covenant, and He chose to create marriage as a picture of His relationship with His people. He takes covenants very seriously and will not break one (1 Chronicles 16:15, Psalm 105:8, Psalm 111:9, Isaiah 54:10), and He does not lie (Numbers 23:19, Titus 1:2). And how does God act as a husband? God promises to never leave us, nor forsake us (Deuteronomy 31:6, Hebrews 13:5). He promises to take care of us and dwell with us (John 14:3). His unfailing love for us will not be shaken (Isaiah 54:10). He is compassionate and gracious, slow to get angry and has abundant love (Psalm 103:8). The list goes on of all the things that God promises those in covenant with him.

So, How Does This Give You A Position To Intercede?

You are in a unique, powerful position to intercede for your spouse and your marriage because of covenant! If your marriage is the very picture of God's relationship with His people, then you can be sure that God is for you and your marriage. He wants to be in covenant with humans, He calls people to be in relationship with Him daily. So, if you are asking for your spouse to return to relationship with God and with you, then you can be sure that He will hear your prayers.

The Victim Gets The Last Say

Additionally, your spouse betrayed YOU. While friends and family may be upset with your spouse, the betrayal was of you. Therefore, when you offer that forgiveness to your spouse and pray for what is best for your spouse, those are POWERFUL words. Yes, God is listening to those friends and family who are praying for your spouse. But when you do it, your words mean more because you are the victim. God listens to the victim who cries out for mercy for her adversary. Think of Jesus praying for those crucifying him (Luke 23:34) and Stephen interceding for those stoning him (Acts 7:60); those prayers are in the Bible as examples to us. It is much easier to pray for mercy for someone who hurt others than for someone who hurt us. God knows that, and that is why if you extend mercy and grace to your spouse by asking God to do the same, He takes notice!

Caution: Free Will Ahead

There is one caution I must share because everything hinges on it. Your spouse has free will. God designed each one of us with the ability to choose to be in relationship with Him or not. It's our choice, no one else can make it for us. God does not force anyone into a relationship with Him. In fact, He is so committed to allowing us to choose for ourselves that He allows us to choose for eternity. If a person does not want to be in relationship with God, he or she will be able to be apart from God for all eternity. So, your spouse has the ability to choose to be in relationship with you as well here on earth. These prayers will not force your spouse to stay and change. But they will create a spiritual atmosphere in which it will be easier to choose God and you and harder to walk away from you both. And that my friends is the power of your prayers.

HOW TO BE IN COVENANT WITH GOD

You picked up this book because you need hope and a miracle. Your spouse has drifted away, and you have nowhere left to turn. You need Someone outside of yourself to change the course of your marriage. My friends, there is Someone who exists who loves you with a love so deep and wide and long that He died so that you could spend eternity with Him. He did not ask you to sacrifice so you could live with Him forever, instead He did the sacrificing. The Creator of the Universe stepped into history and lived a sinless life so that He could be a sacrifice to atone for all of the wrongs that you have committed and will ever commit. This only works because He came back from the dead and is now alive. Really, He is!

However, the catch is that you must accept that Jesus died for your sins, rose from the grave, ascended into heaven and placed His blood on the altar to erase your sins. You must say yes to His offer. Otherwise, when you die *you* will be on the hook to pay for your sins. So, which is it: will you allow Jesus to sacrifice Himself for your sins or would you rather do it yourself? I must tell you that because you haven't been perfect, you won't be able to pay for the wrongs that you have committed. Your blood won't erase your sins. So, in reality, it is Jesus' sacrifice for you or nothing. Sounds pretty obvious, but so many people won't take Him up on his offer. Why? There are a myriad of reasons, but I think many of them boil down to this: they don't want to do what He says. See, when you say yes to Jesus' offer, you agree that He gets to be in charge. But the truth is, He wants only good for you, never harm. He is not like a human who has ulterior motives or selfish decisions, He will always guide you to what is right and best for you.

The benefits of being in covenant with God are endless: living eternally with Him, being able to have joy and peace regardless of your circumstances and wisdom and understanding to live life are just a few. One of the other benefits from being in covenant with God is that you can come before Him and ask for anything. You can be assured that He will hear you and answer you and intervene in your life in crazy, awesome ways. When you pray the prayers listed in this book, they will come before His throne and be a pleasing aroma (Revelation 5:8). The tears you inevitably spill as you are praying will be scooped up, recorded and kept in a container

(Psalm 56:8). And, because you are interceding for your wayward spouse, who has probably wounded you greatly, He will cry with you over the pain and injustice you are experiencing.

So, how do you accept Jesus' offer of covenant so you can come before God day or night with any of your thoughts or requests? You just need to tell Him that you accept His offer. That's it. Many in the American Christian church will go on to say that you need to start reading your Bible and find a Bible believing church. Those things are next steps to learn more about the Creator of the Universe to whom you just pledged your allegiance and to help you discern what He is saying to you (and to know when the voice you hear is NOT Him). But those things are not required to be in covenant with God. It all boils down to relationship!

Talk to God, and let Him talk to you. He may not talk to you with an audible voice though. He may use a verse in the Bible to talk to you, He may use a dream to talk to you or He may use another person to speak His words to you, just to name a few examples. Reading the Bible is so important to know if what you are hearing is actually God talking to you, and being around others who are seeking God helps you grow and stay grounded in the Scriptures, but just remember that neither thing creates your covenant. He is ready right now to be in covenant with you. Just talk to Him!

PRAYERS FOR YOUR WAYWARD SPOUSE

1

Opponents must be gently instructed, in the hope that God will grant them repentance leading them to a knowledge of the truth, and that they will come to their senses and escape from the trap of the devil, who has taken them captive to do his will. 2 Timothy 2:25-26

This was my top go-to verse for my husband because it has it all: a revelation of truth (what truth is AND that he had been deceived) and a successful turning away from the enemy, so he could run back to God, and all because God helped my husband to repent. I filled in his name as I prayed this Scripture. You can do this for your spouse too, and it will go something like this: "Father, grant _____ repentance, leading _____ to a knowledge of the truth, so that _____ will come to his senses and escape from the trap of the devil, who has taken

_____ captive to do his will." God is ready to grant repentance to your spouse, but your spouse must come to God and ask for it. It is there for the taking, but your spouse must take it! The whole reason why we are able to respond to God in the first place is because of His grace, He helps us to see our need for Him and to have the will to turn to Him. Ask God to open that door for your spouse so everything else will fall into place.

2

Pray that your spouse discerns the truth and then that he believes it, acts on it and follows it. Pray that the enemy can no longer blind your spouse. There are so many lies that have been told in your lives and your marriage. According to Jesus Himself, your enemy Satan is the father of lies, he is unable to speak anything other than lies and his mission is to steal from us, kill us and destroy us. But Jesus is the way, the truth and the life (John 14:6). He has come so we can have life and have it to the full (John 10:10). When you ask for your spouse to see, understand, believe and act on truth, you are asking for your spouse to see, understand, believe and act on Jesus!

3

Pray that your spouse has an encounter with the Living God. I have a friend who had a crisis many years ago and lost her hope for a better life. When I asked her how she overcame that time in her life, she said it was because she had "an encounter with the Living God." Pray that for your spouse as well. He needs to be reminded that Someone exists who is larger than his problems and hurts. In the end, God loves your spouse more than anyone else does, including you. Like the story of the prodigal son, God wants your spouse to run back to Him, and He is waiting with open arms. So, ask God to remind your spouse that He exists and is ready to surround your spouse with mercy, grace and restoration.

4

Pray that God gets your spouse's attention and that your spouse hears why. I really like what God told the prophet in the second chapter of Malachi. He said that Judah had been unfaithful, and the Israelites weep and wail because He no longer accepted their offerings. The people wondered why God was displeased, and He explained because He was "acting as a witness between you and the wife of your youth, because you have broken faith with her, though she is your partner, the wife of your marriage covenant." Whew! God takes marriage seriously, and He was upset that men had betrayed their wives. There will come a time in which your spouse will no longer be able to course-correct, but until that time, pray that he hears God calling him.

5

Pray that your spouse operates using the mind of Christ, giving him Jesus' thoughts, feelings, words and actions. If your spouse is in covenant with God, he has the mind of Christ (1 Corinthians

2:16); however, he may not be using Jesus' mind, he may be using his own intellect and feelings, spurred on by his own flesh. Pray that he thinks the way Jesus would think, including understanding people and situations the way that Jesus would. Pray that he feels the emotions that Jesus feels, and not be led by emotions that are born out of his own flesh due to wrong thinking. With Jesus' thoughts and emotions, then pray your spouse has the actions that Jesus would do with the words Jesus would use.

6

Pray that God changes the desires of your spouse's heart and gives him a new way of thinking. Your spouse has desires to do things his way, to follow the god of his own making. He wants his affair partner or his addiction and probably fuels that desire by habitually meditating on those things. Pray that God works a change in your spouse so that his heart does not chase after those things. For me, it was also praying that my husband would feel disgusted and sad when he thought about his affair partner. It would be hard to desire something that disgusts you! This also entailed having a desire for me and our marriage. In Psalm 103:5, David writes that the LORD "satisfies your desires for good things so that your youth is renewed like the eagle's." That is quite a promise, that God will then satisfy you when you desire good things so that you will be full of vim and vigor!

7

Pray that your spouse is no longer conformed to the habits and conventional wisdom of this world but is transformed by the renewing of his mind (Romans 12:2). And what are the patterns of this world? Whatever seems right is right and whatever makes a person feel better is good. These tenets are opposite of God's instructions for us. He is sovereign and has provided a measure of absolute truth for us. We do not have the moral right to decide truth. When you pray this for your spouse, you are asking God to break this old human habit of deciding truth. When your spouse's mind is renewed, he can see what rightly is true.

8

Pray that he has a clean heart and a right spirit. David's cry of wanting a clean heart and a right spirit came after his adultery with Bathsheba was revealed by Nathan the prophet. He writes in Psalm 51: 10-12 "Create in me a pure heart, O God, and renew a steadfast spirit within me. Do not cast me from your presence or take your Holy Spirit from me. Restore to me the joy of your salvation and grant me a willing spirit, to sustain me." Your spouse must be the one to cry out to God, but you can ask God to create such a heart and spirit within him that he speaks these verses over himself. In the meantime, you can pray that your spouse's heart becomes clean and spirit becomes right and ultimately that he finds the joy in being secure in his salvation.

9

Pray that truth is revealed in your home and in your marriage. God loves you and wants both you and your spouse to know, believe and act on truth. However, if your spouse is lying or omitting information (which is still lying), you are missing out on all truth. You need God to reveal all truth in your home and your marriage. For me, God revealed my husband's infidelity in a dream. A few weeks before he disclosed his affair, God gave me a dream that my husband had compromised himself with a woman. As I was telling my husband about the dream the next morning, I felt so terrible because I knew he would never do that to me, and it was borderline accusatory (in my mind) by even vocalizing this dream. Little did I know that God gave me this dream because it was happening. He had warned my husband over and over again to stop, but my husband did not listen. So, God told me.

Why would God intervene? I think God did it for a few reasons. One, He knew that walking down this path would ultimately lead to destruction for my husband, so He told me to bring this into the light to stop this destruction. He knew that I would ultimately intercede for my husband. And two, He did it so that the affair and deception would not increase and hurt us even more than they had

17

already. My husband will tell you that it chilled him that morning listening to my dream because he *knew* that God had intervened. What a way to wake up a wayward spouse! And ever since then, I pray for truth to be revealed in my home. For you it may be seeing a text message, email or online interaction that you would normally not see or overhearing a conversation in a random place. Pray that nothing stays hidden and everything is exposed to the light of truth. This prayer is so powerful in everyday life, even outside of affairs or addictions. We should always want to know, believe and act on truth in all aspects of our lives.

10

Pray physical, emotional, mental and spiritual protection over your spouse. Your spouse is being assaulted in all four realms and probably does not know it. He needs you to intercede for his safety. No one else may be doing so. If your spouse has drifted from God, there is quite a spiritual battle taking place for him. When we are not walking with God, we stray outside His hedge of protection, so your spouse needs your prayers.

Physical protection is the first line of defense, whether it is to protect him from people who would do him harm, such as affair partners or addiction substance suppliers, or to protect him from premature death or injury. Next, emotional and mental protection means that your spouse cannot be influenced by people or situations in an ungodly way, that he has a clear mind and feelings that are appropriate. The last and most vital protection is the spiritual one. As your spouse has wandered, he is already spiritually vulnerable. This spiritual protection can take the form of a believer encountering him and encouraging him with truth or it can be the ability to see a lie for what it is.

11

Pray that your spouse can see the scheme of the enemy from far away and is not fooled again or any longer. Wayward spouses are easy targets for the enemy, who will use the same trick over and over again. Why? Because it works. So, your assignment is to pray that your spouse can see that Trojan horse coming and knows that it is another trick of the enemy. You can be the watchman on his wall, but he has to be willing to let you stand on the wall, be willing to listen to you and be willing to believe you about the threats coming in the distance. My husband was in the military as a young man, and he uses lots of military analogies. Several times in our marriage, he told me that while he does not see anything on the radar, he would be foolish to dismiss my warnings that there was something inbound meant to hurt him.

12

Pray that God writes His name on your spouse's heart, along with all of the truths about your spouse: he is wholly and dearly loved, he is an adopted son and he is chosen, just to name a few (Hebrews 8:10, Revelation 3:12). Pray that the lies from the enemy that have been written on your spouse's heart are erased and are unable to be read. You can be specific here, listing out all of the truths that you know he needs to embrace and lies that you know he needs to have erased.

13

Pray that the spirits of A, B and C are unable to operate around your spouse and in your home. For my husband, it was lust, anger, covenant-breaking, divorce, unforgiveness, fear and bitterness. Whatever your spouse is battling, pray against those things. Want to go a step further? Anoint your home with oil. Oil is representative of the Holy Spirit, and when you anoint your doorposts with oil, you are creating a picture of the Holy Spirit protecting your home from all of the other spirits that you are praying against. When I anointed my home, I went all out by anointing the outside doors (the Holy Spirit protecting the home), inside doors (the Holy Spirit ruling and reigning inside our home) and even his car doors (the Holy Spirit driving his life)! Again, since this is just a symbol, no special oil is needed. I used olive oil because that is what I had.

Then go on to pray that your spouse is *healed* from A, B and C. Few spouses walk away from their marriages or from God who are not disappointed, and disappointment turns into unforgiveness, anger and bitterness. That was my husband, so those were the things I prayed that he was rescued from and ultimately healed from their effects.

14

Pray that your spouse is no longer a person who has some type of religious *something* in his life and that *something* does not make a difference. In 2 Timothy 3:1-5 we read about the last days and how people will be ungodly. At the end of the warning, Paul says that people will have a form of godliness but deny its power. Pray he becomes a man who is serious about his commitment to God and therefore is then able to be serious about his commitment to you as well.

15

Pray that God grants your spouse wisdom. In James 1:5, the brother of Jesus writes that God will give wisdom generously to anyone who asks for it. In the context, James very specifically reminds the reader to believe and not doubt when asking God for wisdom. Your spouse is not asking for wisdom, but you are asking for it on his behalf and you are not doubting that God can give wisdom to him. Your spouse's lack of wisdom is a fundamental reason why he has walked away, so this is a foundational prayer!

16

Pray that your spouse no longer lives a life of regret. When someone does something wrong, God intervenes and lets him know that he was wrong. When a person hides from God because of the embarrassment that comes from missing the mark, then this mental load becomes a problem. Therapists will often characterize the former as "guilt" and the latter as "shame." Both will lead to regret, but the conviction from God will lead a person to repent and run back to Him, while the embarrassment and shame from the enemy will drive a person farther away from God. I wanted my husband to stop focusing on all of the "coulda, woulda, shouldas" of life and be so free in God that his life was now full of doing and being all the things God called him to do and be. He would not "miss out" on anything because he would be walking out the life that God always intended for him to have.

17

Pray that Jesus sets your spouse free and brings His light to your spouse. In Isaiah 61:1, the prophet describes Jesus as coming to proclaim freedom for the captives and release from darkness for the prisoners. Your spouse is being held captive by lies and is moving about in darkness, but God has the keys to the jail cell and a floodlight!

18

Pray that your spouse is free from his chains of trauma. Most people who walk down the road that your spouse is on have some kind of trauma in their background. This was the case for my husband as well. If your spouse has suffered trauma of any kind, list out the traumas and pray he is healed from each of them.

19

Pray for mercy and grace for your spouse. The Scriptures are full of examples of God showing grace and mercy on people who did not deserve it. I have highlighted two Scriptures here because of how they describe God. Psalm 103:8-10 (see below) states flat out that our God is merciful (compassionate) and full of grace. And Psalm 107:17-20 (see below) describes how God healed and rescued people who were suffering because of their own choices to walk away from God! Make no mistake, mercy and grace are not licenses to continue destructive or hurtful behavior. They are ways God infiltrates our world to bring your spouse healing and rescuing: grace is giving us what we don't deserve (healing), and mercy is not giving us what we do deserve (by rescuing us from a life and then eternity without Him).

I talk about this more in Chapter five, but please know that God grieves with you every time your spouse is disrespectful or mistreats you. You are in a unique position to ask God to have mercy and grace on your spouse because you are the one who has been hurt by him. Your intercession in this area is very powerful. Think about Jesus' intercession for those who were supporting His crucifixion or Stephen's intercession for those stoning him. They had the legal right to ask for a delay of consequences so the perpetrators could repent. You have the legal right to do the same.

Psalm 103:8-10 The Lord is compassionate and gracious, slow to anger, abounding in love. He will not always accuse, nor will he harbor his anger forever; he does not treat us as our sins deserve or repay us according to our iniquities.

Psalm 107:17-20 Some became fools through their rebellious ways and suffered affliction because of their iniquities. They loathed all food and drew near the gates of death. Then they cried to the Lord in their trouble, and he saved them from their distress. He sent out his word and healed them; he rescued them from the grave.

20

Pray for justice. You, your spouse and your marriage have been wronged and deserve justice. Everyone thinks of justice as punishment, but there is another side to justice. Justice is also restoring what has been stolen from the victim. In the United States, our justice system includes this portion, such as the restitution that the convicted must make to the victim in terms of a monetary amount to make the victim whole, but we so often overlook it in Scripture. Jesus talked about victims getting justice in the parable and explanation of the persistent widow in the book of Luke. When Phillip overheard the Ethiopian read the scroll of Isaiah in Acts, the Ethiopian was quoting Scripture describing Jesus being deprived of justice. Finally, Psalm 33:5 proclaims that the LORD loves righteousness and justice! If God loves justice, you can be sure that you are in His will when you ask for justice.

I bring this up again in Chapter five when I list prayers that you can pray for yourself, so I will focus here on justice for your spouse. In my marriage I could point to situations and circumstances that set my husband up to believe the lies that came at him. It was still his choice to believe those lies, there is no doubt. But we all know that the enemy fights dirty, and he set up my husband. Emotional stability and innocence were stolen from my husband at a young age, and he, as a robbery victim, deserved justice. He deserved restitution of those things in his life. No, he was not going to go back to be a child and become innocent to the world's evil. But, he could be healed from those childhood traumas that have plagued him and opened him up to believing lies. Your spouse deserves justice as well, and God longs to give it to him.

21

Pray that everything that has been stolen from you, your spouse and your marriage, be restored *with interest*! Remember all the things taken from Job? His oxen, donkeys, sheep, camels, servants and children were literally stolen or killed. But, Job 42:10 tells us that "...the LORD made him prosperous again and gave him twice as much as he had before." Why not pray that for you and your family? Trust, time, respect and intimacy has been stolen. Probably money too. List out everything your spouse, you and your marriage have lost. Give that list to God and ask for everything to be returned *with interest.* All those things can be redeemed!

Let's take intimacy for example. Yes, it can be restored, but the "interest" part of intimacy is the increased amount over what you had in the first place. Same with trust and respect: more than you ever had in your original marriage! So, what about time? God is an expert at redeeming time, meaning that the rest of the time that you are living out is used in a way that is holy and pleasing to Him. The amount of time your marriage has been in disarray can be so much less than the amount of time that your marriage goes on to accomplish great things for God.

22

Pray life over your marriage and describe it as the picture that God intended. What is one picture of marriage in Scripture? Jesus' covenant with believers is described as a picture of a husband and wife in Ephesians, and that is why husbands are commanded to love their wives as Christ loves the church. So, our marriages are symbols of the greater covenant. Ask God to turn your marriage into a living, natural picture of Jesus' relationship with the church. So when people encounter your marriage, they understand the love that God has for His people.

23

Pray that your marriage be restored and redeemed, the marriage God always intended you to have. God had big plans for you and your marriage! And every time we decide to follow our own desires and not obey God, we get farther and farther away from the plan God has for us. So, pray that the ending of this story is a marriage that is better than it has ever been, one that you would have never thought you could ever have! That is the marriage that God intends for you, something so wonderful and loving you can't even picture it.

24

Pray that your spouse sees you the way that God sees you. I often prayed for my husband to love me the way that God loves me. There is no better perception of you than the one that God holds, so you can't go wrong praying this prayer. And, I challenge you to then pray that you see your spouse the way God sees him. God will answer your prayer, and then He will give you more ways to pray for your spouse.

25

Pray that God opens doors to Himself and to you that no affair partner or addiction can shut and shut doors that no affair partner or addiction can open. In other words, pray that nothing stands in the way of your spouse hearing God and taking Him up on His offer of salvation, healing and an abundant life.

26

Pray that you and your spouse have joy and peace. These two things have probably made themselves scarce in your home lately. Both of these things are allowed to be ours if we are in covenant with God, but of course, your enemy tries to steal them from you all the time. Pray that these things return to your home. No one is telling you to be joyful that your marriage may be crumbling, only to hold on to joy as you have faith that God will take care of you no matter what. Peace includes not only safety, but also health, prosperity, favor and wholeness. Sounds like everything you need! When you ask for joy and peace to invade your spirits, strife doesn't have much room to work, allowing God to bring healing (physical, mental, emotional and spiritual) to both of you.

27

Pray that God puts other people in covenant with Him in your spouse's path. Your spouse needs to know and be friends with Jesus followers. It is easier to hear God and be obedient to Him if others in your life are doing the same. If he doesn't have people in his life who know God, pray that God gives your spouse encounters with those people. And anyone who is in your spouse's life for more than a brief encounter should be the same sex as your spouse. The enemy would like nothing more than to wrap up adultery as "something of God," so don't be fooled.

Pray that there is no confusion in relationships that are from God and tremendous confusion in relationships that are not from God. In Scripture, one of the ways God dealt with the enemies of Israel was to throw them into confusion. I wanted all chaos to break out between my husband and his affair partner, and in the meantime, for him to have clarity in our relationship. When Paul is talking about proper decorum in a gathering of believers, he specifies that each person can control his own spirit, as God is not a God of disorder but of peace (1 Corinthians 14:33). If something is from Him, there will be an order and peace to it, but the enemy brings disarray, after the initial enticement of order and peace. So, ask for the confusion to be revealed in what is not from God and for peace and order to settle over your marriage.

Pray for the affair partner. This one may be a tough pill to swallow, but I am going to give you a different perspective. As followers of Jesus, we believe that unless a person is in covenant with God, that person will spend eternity apart from Him. The absence of God is found in the place called Hell, and that is where those who do not choose God will be. The only reason you and I are not headed there is because we took Jesus up on His offer to take the punishment for our sins. So, the affair partner has the same choice, either she or Jesus will pay, and that is a fact that will happen.

Also, what would it look like if the affair partner comes to know Jesus and decides to be in covenant with God? She will never inflict this chaos on another wife, she will see her actions with your husband as they truly are, and she may even apologize to you. It may be your prayers that prevent her from doing this again. Yes, I know that the biggest "churchy" reason to pray this prayer is to save her from a Godless eternity, but it probably takes time and a lot of healing for you to get to that point. If you can remember that she will be a different person when she comes to know Jesus, that may help you open your heart to pray for her as well.

30

Thank God! Can you see any bright side to this chaos in your life? I will never be thankful that my husband had an affair, nor do I think I am scripturally commanded to do so. However, I absolutely see that what the enemy meant for evil, God used for good in my life. For instance, when my whole life was careening out of control, I had to come to the realization that I had control over *nothing* in my life except me. That was a very hard truth for me because I was a very control-oriented person, to my detriment. Let me be clear, God did NOT orchestrate my husband's affair to teach me a lesson. But, He did use the affair to show me that

I had to root out this sin in my life. For some, the praise may be that God revealed the affair or addiction before all of the marriage's assets were stolen. But some of you may be so raw so soon after discovery or disclosure that it may be hard to find something to be thankful for. And if that is you, I encourage you to be honest with God, tell Him that you don't know what to be thankful for in this mess and could He please show you something? He will, I promise.

HAVE GRACE FOR YOURSELF, YOU NEED IT!

You are probably beating yourself up for not paying attention to the "red flags" that were there, for believing your spouse when questioned. Let me tell you a secret: all of those things mean you were a good spouse. Of course you gave your spouse the benefit of the doubt, of course you trusted him. You can't have a marriage long term if there isn't trust. So, give yourself some grace. Your spouse was, or is, a wonderful liar. Very skilled. Do not think you were anything other than a trusting spouse before. You weren't stupid or naive. You were trusting. Your spouse betrayed that trust, so now you must be much more watchful. As you go down this path, you will give strict attention to any additional red flags, which is appropriate. Once your spouse has built up trust over time and through his actions (which is how we all build trust with one another), you will evolve to know what red flags are important to heed and what are just red herrings.

Now, Pray For You

While you are interceding for your spouse, you need to be praying for yourself as well. Your enemy would like nothing better than to take you out of this fight because your prayers are powerful. Don't think you are being selfish or wasting precious prayer time by praying over yourself. We all know that when flight attendants go over the safety procedures before a passenger plane departs, one of the directions they give is to ensure you place your own oxygen mask on before taking care of others around you. If you are with others who are unable to put on their own masks, they will not be able to help you if you run out of oxygen and pass out before you are masked. So please take care of yourself and invite God into your space so you can be a healthy, strong and fearless prayer warrior for your marriage.

Below are prayers that I prayed for myself, and I suspect that they are things that my friends prayed over me too.

1

Be honest with God. Right now, your world may be falling apart, you may struggle to just go to work, and you don't know how you are going to make it to next week. Tell Him that. Tell Him you don't have strength to go on. Tell Him you are scared. Tell Him you feel tired and defeated. Tell Him you feel unloved and abandoned. Whatever it is that you think or feel, tell Him. Then allow Him to tell you that He loves you, you are not abandoned to figure this all out on your own. Allow Him to give you strength and hope that you can get through your present. Well-meaning people say "God won't give you more than you can handle." Garbage. If you could handle everything, you would be God. So, pour out your heart to Him so He can come in and carry you in those places where you can't even lift your head.

2

Pray for justice. In Chapter four, I explained that justice is not just punishment for the perpetrator, but it is also returning everything stolen to the victim, along with interest. You deserve justice, dear friend. God wants to give back to you all the things your spouse stole. Make a list of all of the things that have been taken from you, and for many of you, it starts with your confidence. No matter how small or large, make that list. Then, ask God to return all of those things to you, with interest. What does justice look like on the punishment side? It looks like that whatever your spouse did, he is unable to continue to do it. No more affairs, no more addictions. He is not allowed to continue to hurt you, he must stop his selfish actions. That is justice as well, a protection against further abuses.

Going along with a prayer for justice, David declares that the Lord "works righteousness and justice for all the oppressed" in Psalm 103. This means you! Ask God to work righteousness alongside that justice you are praying for. This means that you are treated well and fairly in all your dealings, that you have a right standing in the eyes of God and in your interactions with humans.

3

Pray for wisdom. You need wisdom as you navigate your situation, and you must ask God to give it to you. Otherwise, you will react with your own thoughts and emotions, which will never lead to a good place. Ask the God who knows everything how to handle everything in your life.

4

Pray for a clean heart and a right spirit. You need to have Jesus' thoughts, emotions, words and actions in order to deal appropriately with your spouse and to make the best decisions. Having a clean heart and a right spirit does not mean you are happy. You are allowed to grieve! It just means that you are trying to see the world, situations and other people with truth, the way Jesus does, and therefore you will think, speak, feel and act accordingly.

5

Pray for mercy and grace. God has such grace and mercy for you, He weeps with you as you weep over how you have been hurt and over your marriage and spouse. Hebrews 4:16 tells us to "approach God's throne of grace with confidence, so that we may receive mercy and find grace to help us in our time of need." This is for you, my friend! God is waiting to hear from you about you, be confident in that, and He can't wait to pour out mercy and grace upon you.

6

Pray to be crowned with love and compassion (Psalm 103:4). What does this even mean? I think it can be taken at least two ways. First, you know intellectually that God has love and compassion for you, and second, when He shows you His love and compassion for you, you acknowledge His goodness to you. God doesn't like that you are mistreated or hurt by anyone. He longs to pour out His love to you so that you know it and can feel it. When you are in a marriage where your spouse, the person who is supposed to be closest to you, isn't loving to you, let God show you His love.

7

Pray that you are humble under God's authority, so He can bring a right to your wrongs at the correct time. 1 Peter 5:6 states "Humble yourselves, therefore, under God's mighty hand, that he may lift you up in due time." I love this prayer for myself, that I stay in obedience (be humble) and in His shelter and then He will exalt me (bring justice) when the time is right. When I am lifted up, I triumph over my enemies and walk in victory.

8

Pray for protection. In Chapter four, you prayed for physical, emotional, mental and spiritual protection over your spouse, and now it is time to pray it over yourself as well. I heard Pastor Charles Stanley on the radio years ago speak about when we are most vulnerable to attack by the enemy, and it can be summed up in the acronym HALT: Hungry, Angry, Lonely and Tired. These represent the physical, emotional and mental states of vulnerability, which so often usher in the spiritual attack. You have taken on a great spiritual battle, and you must wrap yourself in prayers if you want to see the end.

9

Pray for your own healing. Regardless of whether you have previous hurts, what you are going through now is a very intense trauma from which you need to be healed. You previously prayed for physical, emotional, mental and spiritual protection; pray now for physical, emotional, mental and spiritual healing. This trauma touches all of those areas, and you need to be delivered from the trauma. I love Psalm 107:17-20 because in those verses God describes people who through their own actions became sick. It was their fault they were ill. And God healed them, even though it was their own fault. If God has compassion on people who disobeyed Him and because of that need a healing, how much more compassion will He have on you who have been hurt through someone else's actions?

10

Pray protection from the very thing your spouse is going through. If your spouse committed adultery, pray that you reject all inappropriate attention and affection from others; if your spouse is an addict, pray that you reject use of any substance that will lead to harm. It may seem crazy, but as you intercede for your spouse in the area of his downfall, you are more prone to attack there.

11

Pray for a support system in your life. I talk about this more in Chapter six, but you need to find others who have gone through the same thing with their spouses. Pray that you are directed to the right people and/or organization.

Thank God!

Thank God and recognize that He will take care of you, no matter what happens. One big step of faith for me was when I thought back to God's rescue of the Israelites from Egypt, how hundreds of thousands of people wandered in the desert for decades, and their clothes and shoes did not wear out (Deuteronomy 29:5). Not knowing how I would upkeep my home if our marriage ended, I asked God to ensure that the fixtures in my home did not wear out, or if they did, that I would have the money for any repairs. In my mind, that was such a game changer! I had the right to ask that request because I am in covenant with God. And I truly believed that He could do that for me. It allowed me to let go of some fear and hold on to some faith. Ask God to show you what you need to know to replace fear with faith. He will, I promise!

RESOURCES

Friends

Surround yourself with people who love you and will pray for you. If you are interceding for your spouse, you must also have people who are interceding for you. If you have friends you can trust and are in covenant with God, please ask them to pray for you, your spouse and your marriage. You do not need to give all the gory details. In fact, please do not. But, tell your friends how you want them to pray. For example, "I need you to pray that my spouse starts listening to God," or "I need you to pray that I have wisdom and discern truth."

But, there is a downside with friends. Your friends mean well, they really do, but if they have never walked down the path you are walking, they tend to have a black and white way of viewing your journey. Most friends have no room for anything other than 100% perfect from your spouse. And that won't happen. I would bet that before you found yourself in this situation, if you had ever thought about being in this situation, your response would have been, "I would walk out the door and not look back." But, lo and behold, here you are. Why? Because it is easy to make declarations until you need to live by them. So, please be wise in what specifics you share.

Affair Recovery

affairrecovery.com

It is paramount that you find a support system of people of the same sex who have also gone down this path or are on the path currently. Affair Recovery is one of those places where you can find other betrayed spouses who want to heal from the affairs their partners had. This organization has pay resources for the betrayed spouse (Harboring Hope), the unfaithful spouse (Hope for Healing) and couples. In addition, there are lots of free resources on its website and its Youtube channel.

After prayer, Affair Recovery was the single most important tool in my toolbox to get through the pain of adultery. And, believe it or not, my husband recommended it to me! He had come across the Hope for Healing course for the unfaithful and was going to enroll and found the Harboring Hope for betrayed spouses at the same time. This group was a lifesaver for me. Led by a woman who had been in our shoes, six women, including myself, from all across the country had a group phone call for 13 weeks, going through the proprietary workbook. After the 13 weeks ended, five of us decided to continue to talk, and we met online weekly for two more years, then every other week for another year and a half. These ladies were my lifeline! We understood one another's triggers, hurts and hopes. And, contrary to what many may think, these ladies were the biggest supporters of each other's husbands as well. No, they never excused bad behavior, they would call it out; however, they understood that victories come in steps and patience is important. Some people may be deterred by the cost of the class; Affair Recovery did offer scholarships, and it may be worth contacting the organization to find out if it still does. You absolutely need to surround yourself with others in your shoes.

Dr. Joe Beam And Marriage Helper

marriagehelper.com

This organization also has pay and free resources, including on YouTube. The focus of this organization is to restore broken marriages. (Dr. Beam's story is quite the tale of betrayal, and you may think that if his marriage can be restored, yours can be as well!) Even if your spouse is not on board, please check out the website and YouTube channel to glean what you can for yourself.

Codependents Anonymous

CoDA.org

This organization has brought a lot of healing

to people near and dear to me. There are in-person and online meetings all over the nation. People I know who have participated in CoDA meetings tell me that each group has its own personality, so if the concept is something you want to explore in your life, but the group seems "off" in any way, look for another group.

Therapy

Seriously consider talking to a professional. If your spouse will not go to couples counseling with you, think about finding a counselor for just yourself. But if you can afford it, don't be afraid to do both types of therapy. Here are a couple of cautions for you. Please know that not all counselors have expertise in this field, and even if they do, they may not be the right professional for you. If the counselor does not resonate with you, find someone else. I had a counselor (for a few sessions) who didn't seem to understand the emotional affair my husband had and where that left us in our marriage. Time to find a new counselor! Also, if you want to save your marriage if possible, you will need to find a counselor who will have that goal as well. If not, the counselor will see you walking away as just as valid an option as staying is. If you choose to go to therapy, just know you may see a few counselors before finding the right fit for you and your situation.

Dr. Kenneth Adams

Dr. Adams wrote the book *When He's Married to Mom*, a guide for men who are emotionally enmeshed with their mothers and for the women who are married to those men. While being enmeshed with their mothers is not the only reason why men commit adultery, it is a common reason. If you think this may be your spouse, this book is worth reading. You can find it on Amazon.

Spiritual Guidance

When my life fell apart with the disclosure of my husband's affair, I ran to God for help. There were several pastors/evangelists that I sought out to read their articles or listen to their podcasts on YouTube. None are experts on marriage, they just happen to be good Bible teachers. I learned so much about God's character and His view of me, along with a better understanding of Scripture from these teachers. I urge you to make your own list of channels on YouTube or of specific websites to visit regularly to ensure you are getting solid teaching on God and Scriptures.

In the end, remember friends that you are not crazy and you are not alone. Your Father in Heaven loves you and loves your spouse. There is hope!

ABOUT THE AUTHOR

M K Clark

MK Clark grew up in the Midwest before moving to the Southwest with her husband. Her favorite place is "outside," and she can be found running, hiking, kayaking or reading on the porch when she is not working at her day job. Because she has never come across anyone in this world who doesn't need some encouragement, it is MK's mission to be an encourager to others.

www.ingramcontent.com/pod-product-compliance
Lightning Source LLC
Chambersburg PA
CBHW062127040426
42337CB00044B/4382